JUN '93

CH

THE
APACHE
INDIANS

THE JUNIOR LIBRARY OF
AMERICAN INDIANS

THE
APACHE
INDIANS

Nicole Claro

CHELSEA HOUSE PUBLISHERS

New York   Philadelphia

FRONTISPIECE: An Apache basketmaker, photographed in the late 1800s.

CHAPTER TITLE ORNAMENT: A masked dancer, adapted from a painted figure on an Apache medicine man's shirt.

Chelsea House Publishers
EDITOR-IN-CHIEF Richard S. Papale
MANAGING EDITOR Karyn Gullen Browne
COPY CHIEF Philip Koslow
PICTURE EDITOR Adrian G. Allen
ART DIRECTOR Maria Epes
ASSISTANT ART DIRECTOR Howard Brotman
MANUFACTURING MANAGER Gerald Levine
SYSTEMS MANAGER Lindsey Ottman
PRODUCTION MANAGER Joseph Romano
PRODUCTION COORDINATOR Marie Claire Cebrián

The Junior Library of American Indians
SENIOR EDITOR Liz Sonneborn

Staff for THE APACHE INDIANS
COPY EDITOR Martin Mooney
EDITORIAL ASSISTANT Michele Berezansky
DESIGNER Debora Smith
PICTURE RESEARCHER Vicky Haluska
COVER ILLUSTRATOR Vilma Ortiz

First Printing
1 3 5 7 9 8 6 4 2

Library of Congress Cataloging-in-Publication Data

Claro, Nicole.
  The Apache Indians/by Nicole Claro.
    p. cm.—(The Junior library of American Indians)
  Includes bibliographical references and index.
  Summary: Examines the history, culture, and future prospects of the Apache Indians.
  ISBN 0-7910-1656-0
  1. Apache Indians—Juvenile literature. [1. Apache Indians.
2. Indians of North America.] I. Title. II. Series.
E99.A6C49 1992   91-37339
970.004'972—dc20   CIP
                                                       AC

CONTENTS

This war shield was painted by Geronimo, the famed Apache warrior.

CHAPTER 1

The Battle of the Animals

Long ago, the world was always dark. There were no humans on the earth. However, many creatures lived here—huge beasts and long serpents who were always hungry. To ease their hunger, they feasted on weaker creatures. The small animals—birds, rabbits, and squirrels—could not escape because of the eternal darkness.

One day, all of the creatures began to argue. Should the world remain dark or should there be daylight? Of course, the fierce beasts wished for darkness so they could continue to prey on the gentler ones, who wanted light.

To settle the matter, the animals agreed to play a guessing game. The large creatures would form one team and the small ones the other. Each team would hide some sticks in holes burrowed in the ground. The first team to guess where the other had hidden all its sticks would be the winner. The winning team would then be allowed to kill the losers.

At first, the contest was close. But as the beasts moved ahead, the small creatures began to panic. Their last hope was Turkey. At the beginning of the game, he had wandered off to take a nap. His teammates found him and woke him so he could join in the game. A skilled player, Turkey found all of the beasts' remaining sticks except for one. The black sky then opened up and, for the first time, daylight bathed the earth. Just as Wren chirped, "Daybreak is coming," the small animals discovered the beasts' final stick.

The winners immediately descended on the losers. The birds among the small creatures took on Giant, the fiercest of the beasts. They shot arrow after arrow but could not kill him. Lizard, himself one of the beasts, then joined the birds in their revenge. He knew that Giant's heart lay on the bottom of his foot. With one carefully aimed

A view of the Chiricahua Mountains in the beautiful Apache homeland.

arrow, Lizard struck Giant in the heart, killing him instantly. This is why there are no giants today.

Seeing Giant's fate, the other beasts fled in terror. The birds flew after them, shooting arrows at their enemies. They almost pierced Snake before he slithered away into

the cracks of the mountains, where the birds could not follow him. This is why snakes still inhabit the desert.

This story has long been told by the Apache people. It explains some of their ideas about how the Apache homeland came to be as it is today. But the tale tells something more. It also suggests how the Apaches view the world and their place in it.

For hundreds of years, the Apaches have lived in the American Southwest. In this harsh desert environment, it was difficult to survive. Just to find enough food, they had to work hard, constantly moving from one place to another in search of wild plants and animals. Like the small creatures in the story, the Apaches always had to be alert to possible dangers. The small animals had to be ever watchful of the large creatures. The Apaches had to guard themselves against the often hostile forces of nature.

The Apaches were challenged by more than their environment. Throughout their history, they have also been threatened by various peoples—Spaniards, Mexicans, Americans, and other Indian groups. To protect themselves and their territory, the Apaches became talented and fearless fighters, ready to use their strength to defeat any foe. Like the small creatures, they often had to rely on their intelligence and fierceness to survive battles against larger and more powerful enemies.

Much has happened to the Apache people since they first began to tell of the contest in the animal world between the large and the small. The Apaches themselves have endured many contests. Some they won. Others they lost. In the course of these struggles, they had to abandon many of their old ways. Yet their fighting spirit remains. Over time, the Apaches' foes have changed, but their willingness to take on any enemy, despite the odds, is as strong as ever. ◣

A shaman named Jim, photographed in the late 1800s.

CHAPTER **2**

A Mighty People

The Apaches did not always live in the Southwest. Once they lived far to the north in what is now Alaska and northwestern Canada. Sometime long ago, they left this cold region and traveled south. No one knows exactly when or why.

The Apaches eventually settled in a large area in the center of the present-day United States. The area stretched from what is now Kansas and Oklahoma to the portion of Arizona just above the Mexican border. The Indians were scattered throughout this territory, living in groups of about 200 people called *bands*. Not all of these bands got along well at all times. Still they considered themselves one people.

Unlike their neighbors the Pueblos, the Apaches did not build villages. Instead, they lived in tipis or wickiups. *Tipis* were cone-shaped dwellings covered with animal hides. *Wickiups* were circular huts made of branches and grasses.

Both of these types of houses could be easily taken down, transported to another place, and put up again. They suited the Apaches because they were constantly moving from place to place in search of food. Their land was not very fertile, so they did little farming. Instead, the Apaches obtained most of their food by hunting. They had to follow animal herds wherever they went.

Using bows and arrows, Apache men stalked antelopes, deer, hares, and even rodents. Some bands also hunted buffalo. These animals were not only a food source. They also provided skins, which the Apache women sewed into clothing.

Women wore fringed skirts. Men dressed in *breechcloths*. These garments were made of a strip of animal skin tucked between the legs and held in place at the waist by a belt. Both men and women wore knee-high moccasins. The upturned toes of these durable shoes caused the Comanches, another Indian people, to call the

An Apache family sitting outside their wickiup — a portable house made of branches and grass.

Apaches the "Ta-ashi." This word meant "turned-up" in the Comanches' language.

Apache women had other important duties aside from making clothes. They gathered fruits, vegetables, nuts, and berries that grew wild in their lands. They did most of the cooking and often tracked small animals, such as rabbits. Child rearing was also the responsibility of women, although they sometimes received help from men.

Family life was very important to the Apaches. Many relatives—parents, grandparents, children, uncles, and aunts—built their wickiups close together. When an Apache couple married, they would come to live near the wife's family. If the wife died, the husband would keep close ties with her relatives. Usually, he would even marry one of her sisters or cousins.

The Apaches did not have a permanent government to make rules and laws. Instead, whenever a day-to-day problem arose, several families would form a council. Any man noted for his bravery, wealth, or wisdom could attend. At the council, the men would discuss the problem and together find a solution.

Larger questions, such as whether to go to war, were answered by band councils. Some men in these councils inherited their positions. Others were awarded them after performing an act of great courage in a raid or a war.

In a raid, Apache warriors attacked the camp of another group of Indians. Their goal was to steal food or other important goods. Sometimes, raiders also took captives.

Raiding was a risky act. But warfare was even more dangerous. The Apaches usually went to war to avenge the death of war-

ORIGINAL HOMELANDS OF THE APACHES

(modern state and international boundaries)

riors killed during raids. Such battles were led by the relatives of the slain raiders.

When a person died, his or her relatives went into mourning. They were thought to be too sad to help with the funeral. People from other families, therefore, were responsible for placing the body and the dead person's personal possessions on a horse. The horse was led high into the mountains. There the body was hidden and the possessions destroyed. The people then killed the horse and returned to their dwellings. Once at home, they cleansed their bodies and burned their clothes.

Most Apaches believed in and feared the ghosts of the dead. They thought that there were two places a person's ghost might go. One place was for the ghosts of good people. The other was for the ghosts of witches. But a ghost could go nowhere if a funeral were not performed. The Apaches held these ceremonies as soon as possible. Otherwise, the ghost might stay on earth and do harm to the living.

The Apaches also believed in spiritual power. This power was everywhere. It was in every object, idea, and person. Certain chosen people were thought to have the ability to control spiritual power. They were called *shamans*.

Power could be used for good or evil. But shamans most often used it to cure illnesses. They performed many different ceremonies to heal the sick. <—

In one, the shaman blew tobacco smoke to the north, south, east, and west. Then he called upon his power to aid the patient. This ceremony would be repeated four nights in a row. At the end of the fourth night, the shaman would put his mouth on the patient's body and suck out the poison that was believed to have caused the illness. Sometimes he would also give the patient special instructions or a charm to help her or him get better.

In another ceremony, the patient first had to ask for the shaman's help. Then, the shaman and four masked men danced and sang to the rhythm of drumbeats. After four nights of dancing, the healer again told the patient to do certain things to ensure the recovery.

Other ceremonies were held on more joyous occasions than death and disease. Among the most important of these were performed when a girl or a boy reached puberty. These ceremonies were meant to welcome young people into adulthood.

A girl's puberty ceremony was held in a special tipi made just for the occasion. For

four days, people gathered there. In the morning, a female shaman and the girl painted each other with pollen. Dancing and singing followed. On the final day, a singer painted the girl with white clay. She then walked on an animal skin along a path of pollen. The audience ended the ceremony

The painting on this animal hide depicts a girl's puberty ceremony.

by knocking down the tipi and tossing small presents in the air for the local children. When the ceremony was over, the girl was considered a woman. Four days later, she became eligible for marriage.

A boy prepared for marriage by becoming a warrior. His father and uncles began his training early. He first learned to run fast and perform great feats of strength. He then accompanied his elders on raids. If a boy proved himself an able raider and warrior, he was taught a special sacred language. Only after he had mastered this tongue could he get married.

Each band performed these ceremonies in its own way. But behind all Apache ceremonies was one central idea. This was the belief that power came from the earth, sky, and water and that this power was great. Even the most fierce Apache warrior bowed to the force of nature.

In the 1500s, the Apaches would meet people who did not share their respect for this higher power. These people thought nature should be battled and destroyed. Their ideas would baffle the Apaches, just as the Apaches' beliefs would confuse their new acquaintances. Their meeting—especially the clash of their ideas about the world— would change the Indians' lives forever. ▲

Spanish explorer
Don Francisco Vás-
quez de Coronado
was one of the first
non-Indians to meet
the Apaches.

CHAPTER 3

Spanish Strangers

In 1527, explorer Pánfilo de Narváez confidently left Spain with 5 ships and 600 men. The Spanish government had given him permission to travel across the Atlantic Ocean to North America. Narváez hoped to find gold there. He also intended to claim land on the continent for Spain.

The explorer never had the chance to fulfill either goal. Disease and storms killed him and almost all of his men while they crossed the ocean. Only four survived. Nine years after leaving their homeland, these men stumbled into Mexico City. The Spaniards in this bustling settlement were amazed by the stories they had to tell.

23

The survivors explained that, after reaching the shore, they were taken captive by strange people they called Indians. After six years, they finally managed to escape. They then began a long trek through the dry, hot land of what is now Texas to territory settled by the Spanish in Mexico. Along the way, they met more Indians. Some of these Indians were Apaches. They had never before met white people. But instead of being frightened, they offered friendship to the four exhausted men. The Indians even helped guide them to the city.

Most impressive to the survivors' listeners was a fantastic story told to them by their Indian friends. The Indians explained that there were seven cities nearby that contained unbelievable riches. The cities were supposedly filled with gold. Their walls, the Indians related, glittered with emeralds.

The viceroy (the top Spanish official in Mexico) was delighted when he heard this story. He asked several men to go in search of the seven cities. Among them was a missionary, Fray Marcos de Niza, and a black slave, Estavanico.

When the group reached the village of Vacapan, its members stopped to celebrate Easter. A black slave named Estavanico was sent ahead to scout the region. He was told to travel no farther than 150 miles from Vacapan. If Estavanico saw anything exciting, he was to send back a cross the size of his palm.

Soon, an enormous cross arrived in the village. The Spaniards knew Estavanico must have come upon something spectacular. Some set off to find the slave. They traveled through many Apache camps where Estavanico had been. There they learned that he had pressed on, journeying much farther north than he had been instructed.

The search for the slave ended near Hawikuh, in the present-day state of New Mexico. Hawikuh was a *pueblo*—a village of houses made from a clay called adobe. The Zuni, a branch of the Pueblo Indians, lived there. They were frightened by their visitor. The Zuni knew that foreign people had conquered and destroyed other Indian groups. Convinced that he intended to hurt them, the Indians murdered the slave.

After learning of Estavanico's fate, the travelers returned to Mexico. Even though they had not entered the pueblo, Niza claimed that Hawikuh was covered with jewels. Their reports convinced the viceroy that they had found one of the seven fabulous cities.

He then sent an army of 1,600 men, led by Don Francisco Vásquez de Coronado, to Hawikuh. As the group neared the village, Coronado sent messages ahead, saying the Spaniards came in peace. The Zuni did not believe the foreigners.

An angry Coronado directed his men to storm the pueblo. They defeated the Zuni but took little pleasure in the victory. They searched the village, but found no jewels and no gold. The exciting reports about Hawikuh had all been lies.

Although disappointed, Coronado did not give up. He journeyed to six more pueblos looking for the cities of treasure. Along the way he met a group of Apaches camped at the mouth of the Rio Grande. The Spaniard was impressed by their intelligence and described them as "gentle people, faithful in their friendships."

All of the pueblos Coronado came upon were like Hawikuh. Although impressive in size, they contained none of the riches the Spaniards were hoping to find. Coronado finally declared his mission a failure.

His men left the lands of the Apaches and the Pueblos. But their influence lived on. The Spaniards had things—such as guns, cattle, and horses—that the Indians wanted. And the Indians had other goods—

such as buffalo hides and corn—that the Spaniards wanted. The two groups began to trade with each other at posts in northern Mexico.

The Spaniards did not treat the Pueblos well. They often beat and robbed them. Generally, they had more respect for the Apaches. But when the Spaniards began to capture Apaches to serve as their slaves, their good relations crumbled. The Apache warriors then did not hesitate to fight back.

From the late 1600s to the late 1700s, the Apaches attacked many Spanish settlements in Mexico. Nearly 4,000 Spaniards

In 1846, the United States went to war with Mexico. With their victory, the Americans gained control of a great deal of Mexican land, including Apache country.

were killed in these battles. The Apaches also stole or destroyed millions of dollars worth of property.

In 1786, the viceroy, Bernardo de Gálvez, decided something had to be done to stop the Apaches. Instead of fighting the Indians, he suggested giving them gifts of food and other goods. The viceroy believed the Apaches would then not need or want to steal from the Spanish.

Gálvez died a few months after taking office. His replacement, Manuel Antonio Flores, was not interested in a peaceful solution to the Spaniards' problems with the Indians. He sent more troops than ever into Apache territory. Some Apaches fled just north of the Mexican border to present-day Arizona. But more continued the attacks.

In 1789, yet another viceroy, Conde de Revillagigedo, decided to put Gálvez's plan back in motion. The Spanish government once again provided food and clothing for the Apaches. Peace was maintained for the next 100 years until the government determined that giving goods to the Indians was too expensive. To pay for the provisions, it began to tax the Spanish settlers. Not wanting their money spent on the Apaches, they refused to pay these taxes. The Apaches' supplies decreased and the Indians became furious. Soon there was more blood-shed.

Officially, the Mexican government still favored peaceful relations with the Apaches. But in reality, Mexico had become a violent and confusing land. The settlers were not only fighting the Indians. They were also battling among themselves. Some settlers wanted Mexico to be independent from Spain. Others remained loyal to their home country. After years of killing, Mexico became an independent nation in 1821.

But the violence was still far from over. In 1846, Mexico went to war with the United States over control of Texas. The United States won, and the peace treaty forced Mexico to surrender a huge amount of land. This included Apache territory in what is now northern New Mexico and Arizona. In the treaty, the United States also agreed to prevent the Apaches from traveling south and raiding Mexican settlements.

For more than 200 years, the Apaches had struggled to protect their homeland from the Spanish. Now they suddenly had to deal with different intruders—Americans. Although the faces of their enemies had changed, the battle for their home would continue. ▲

Geronimo, the great Apache leader, battled the U.S. Army for years because he refused to live on a reservation.

CHAPTER **4**

Fighting Americans

The American Southwest saw many changes in the mid-1800s. Americans from the East rushed to the area. Some wanted to settle in the vast region the United States had just acquired from Mexico. Others hoped to become rich by mining gold and other valuable minerals. But few had any concern for the area's original residents. The Americans thought this land was theirs, even though Indians had lived on it for hundreds of years.

Many Indian groups fought these new-comers. But no others defended lands from invasion as fiercely as the Apaches. They

31

had a long history as superior warriors. They battled their new enemy with the same passion with which they had fought the Spaniards and Mexicans before them. Even so, the Americans kept coming. As their numbers increased, the Southwest became ever more violent.

One branch of the Apaches—the Mescaleros—decided that the fighting was out of control. In 1850, they told James S. Calhoun, the governor of New Mexico Territory, that they wanted peace. The next year, Calhoun signed a treaty with the leaders of the Mescaleros and the Jicarillas (another Apache branch). In it, both sides promised not to stage any more attacks.

Calhoun was pleased with the peace. He wanted to make treaties with still more Indians, especially the powerful Warm Springs Apaches. Calhoun's plan, however, was blocked by an army officer named Edwin Vose Sumner. Sumner despised the Apaches and wanted the army's war with the Indians to continue. Against Calhoun's wishes, he instructed his men to build new forts, many on Apache land. The Apaches were displeased. The new forts could only mean that the army was preparing for more battles.

continued on page 41

FROM THE SKINS OF ANIMALS

The meat of wild animals traditionally provided the Apaches with most of their food. But almost as important to the Indians were the animals' skins. From skins, the Apaches made all their clothing, including dresses, moccasins, shirts, and robes. They also used skins to create ceremonial headdresses and masks and war shields.

Men were responsible for hunting. However, women were in charge of the equally difficult task of turning animal skins into leather. This time-consuming process is called tanning.

An Apache woman's first step in tanning a hide was to scrape all the flesh off the skin using a bone tool. Next, she rubbed the skin with a paste made of animal fat and brains until it became soft. Finally, she stretched the skin and allowed it to dry.

Often, the Apaches went one step further and painted the tanned leather. With dyes made from vegetables and tree bark, they created beautiful designs long admired by Indians and non-Indians alike.

White Mountain Apache made the attached quiver and bow case shown here. The practice of joining the two items originated with the Chiricahua.

Crosses often symbolized
the four prime directions.
The mask at top left has a
decorative cross-shaped
attachment made of
deerskin. On the mask at
left, crosses are inscribed
within circles.

Some Apache warriors attached antelope horns to their headdresses.

Eagle feathers top this warrior's headdress, which was held in place by a beaded chin strap.

The hide garment at left shows mirror images of masked figures and serpents. The skin at center depicts masked dancers circling a fire before three rings of observers.

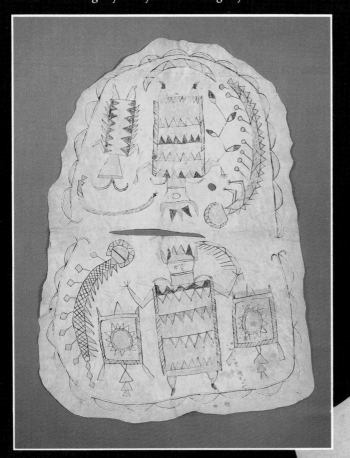

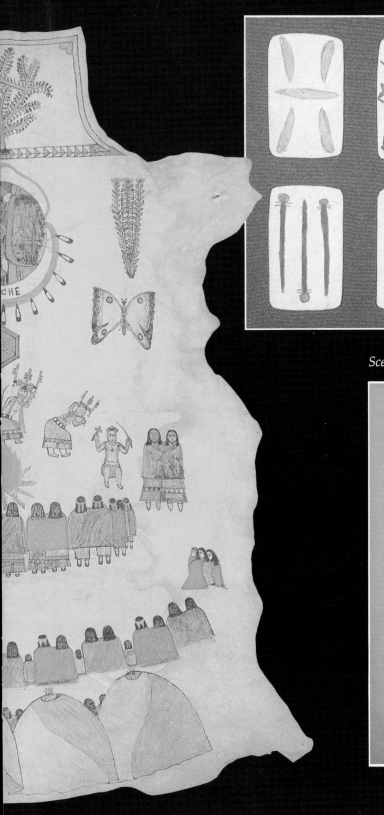

Whites introduced playing cards to the Apache, who developed a rawhide deck faced with stick figures instead of numbers. The exact meaning of these pictographs is unknown.

Scenes of daily life adorn the skin at lower right.

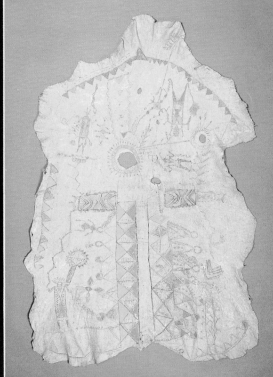

A Mescalero woman sewed this fringed and beaded dress.

This painted bag with shoulder strap was made by a Chiricahua.

Even in cold weather, Apache men needed freedom of movement and thus wore round-necked, fringed tunics.

Shields made of cowhide were wetted and molded into shape, and then hardened over coals. A century plant adorns this painted shield.

continued from page 32

Another incident made the Apaches certain that the Americans had no intention of keeping the peace. A white-owned company built a gold mine on the lands of the Warm Springs Apaches without consulting the Indians first. One of their leaders, Mangas Coloradas, went to speak with the miners. Although he did not like or trust non-Indians, he wanted to deal with them fairly. He politely asked the miners to leave Apache territory. He even told them of a specific place farther south where he knew there were richer deposits of gold. The miners responded to Mangas's modest request by tying him up and whipping him.

The Apaches were furious about how Mangas had been treated. In anger, they raided mail carriages, wagon trains, and army camps. The army blamed Mangas for all the trouble and decided to capture him. Claiming they wanted to talk about a peace treaty, a group of soldiers tricked him into traveling to an army camp unarmed. There, Mangas was tortured, shot, and scalped.

Of course, Mangas's murder just made the Apaches' attacks more fierce than ever. Their raids increased. So did the Americans' bloody retaliations.

Perhaps the most horrifying incident occurred at Camp Grant, a U.S. army post in

present-day Arizona. In February 1871, the Aravaipa Apaches arrived at the camp. They asked the officer in charge, Lieutenant Royal Emerson Whitman, if they could live nearby. The Indians explained that they had been hiding in the mountains because they were afraid the army wanted to attack them. However, the winter in the mountains had been brutal. Many Aravaipas had died in the freezing temperatures. The survivors said that they meant the soldiers at Camp Grant no harm. They wanted only to return to their old home on the Aravaipa Creek, where they could live more comfortably.

Thousands of prospectors searching for gold invaded the Apaches' territory in the mid-1800s.

Whitman felt for the exhausted and hungry Aravaipas. He told them that they could stay near the camp. He offered them some food and also gave them permission to gather the wild plants in area. The Aravaipas were grateful. They knew the lieutenant's kindness had saved many of their lives.

Unfortunately, settlers in the nearby town of Tucson were not so charitable. The Apaches had raided Tucson many times. Many whites there understandably hated the Indians. They were not pleased to hear that the soldiers at Camp Grant were extending aid to their worst enemies.

Whitman found out that some men from Tucson were coming to the post to attack the Aravaipas. He tried to warn the Indians, but his messengers were too late. The Tucson citizens had already set upon the Apaches as they slept. They shot or clubbed to death more than 100 people, mostly women and children. The 29 children who survived were taken as captives. Most were later sold as slaves in Mexico.

Ulysses S. Grant, the president of the United States, was shocked. He demanded that the mob from Tucson be tried in court. More than 100 men were brought to trial. But all were declared innocent. Unlike the president, the members of the juries did not want to see the mob punished. They, too, had suffered the Apaches' attacks and approved of the men's massacre of the defenseless Aravaipas.

President Grant was disturbed by the outcome of the trials. It helped to persuade him to create a new government policy regarding Indians. Grant's peace policy was designed to end the wars between Indians and whites in the Southwest once and for all. According to his plan, certain tracts of land—called *reservations*—would be given to Indians. Whites would not be allowed to settle in these areas.

The government had been creating reservations for many years. The Apaches had been given several, but the arrangement had never worked well. Because the Apaches were hunters, they needed to be able to follow animal herds wherever they roamed in order to feed themselves. When they were required to stay inside small reservations, hunting was impossible. Reservation Apaches then had to rely on the government to give them food. The government promised them food in exchange for agreeing to live on a reservation. But the Indians were never given enough. Hungry and sick, the Apaches grew to hate reservation life.

An engraving of Apache warriors raiding a stagecoach.

Grant had a plan to make reservations better places to live. He maintained that the Indians should be taught to farm. If they could grow their own crops, they would not need food from the government. Grant, however, did not take into consideration that the Apaches loved the hunt. They had little interest in becoming settled farmers.

General George Crook tried to force the Apaches to live on reservations.

In 1871 and 1872, the Apaches were granted four reservations. Some Indians agreed to move to these areas. But many more refused. They knew what reservations were like and wanted nothing to do with them.

The government decided to make the Apaches settle on reservations by force. Troops led by General George Crook were sent out to fight the Indians. Outnumbered, many of the Apache bands surrendered and agreed to move.

Immediately, it became clear that the new reservation plan would not work well. The government placed many bands on each reservation. Although Indians of all bands considered themselves Apaches, they did not always get along. Unhappily confined to a small area, the different bands began to fight among themselves.

Not all branches of the Apaches were defeated by Crook. The Chiricahuas, for instance, successfully resisted the army's campaign against them. They had long been at war with the United States. This war began in October 1860, years before Grant even created his peace policy.

In that month, a group of Apaches raided the ranch of the Ward family in present-day Arizona. In addition to livestock, the Indians seized the Wards' 12-year-old son, Felix. His father was convinced that the Chiricahuas were responsible. He asked the U.S. Army to help retrieve his boy from these Indians.

Second lieutenant George Bascom traveled to Chiricahua country and set up camp. Soon, a Chiricahua leader, Cochise, arrived at the camp to discuss the Ward affair. His wife, two children, and three warriors (who were probably also his relatives) came with him. Bascom and Cochise entered the soldier's tent and immediately the lieutenant accused Cochise of stealing the Wards' boy. Cochise calmly replied that he and the Chiricahuas had had nothing to do with the raid.

However, the leader added that he would be happy to try to find out which band had and to help recover Felix. Even though Cochise was well known for his honesty, Bascom would not believe him. He ordered the soldiers who were surrounding the tent to rush in and capture Cochise. The Apache leader reacted quickly. He pulled out a knife and slit a hole in the tent through which, in a hail of gunfire, he was able to escape.

Cochise's relatives were not so lucky. They were held captive by the soldiers. Cochise asked Bascom to release them. The soldier refused. He told Cochise the captives would be free to go only after he returned Felix to his parents. Cochise again explained he did not know where the boy was, but Bascom would not listen.

After the meeting, Cochise became convinced Bascom would kill his relatives. In desperation, he had his warriors raid a stagecoach and take four Americans aboard hostage. Cochise then sent a message to Bascom, offering to exchange the hostages for his relatives. When Bascom did not respond, Cochise became enraged. He told his men to torture the four Americans to death. When the soldiers found out what had happened, they killed the three warriors they had been holding prisoner.

The U.S. Army built forts on Apache land to protect Americans from Indian attacks.

After the "Cut the Tent Affair," the Chiricahuas and the Americans became sworn enemies. For many years, they staged bloody attacks on one another. As more and more people were killed, the two sides' hatred grew stronger.

In 1872, Cochise decided that the war had gone on long enough. He signed a peace treaty with the U.S. government. In it, the Chiricahua agreed to move to a reservation. But, unlike most Apaches, they would not have to leave their homeland. Cochise made sure that their reservation would be in their own territory.

Two years later, Cochise died. The government then decided it no longer needed to honor the treaty they had made with the great leader. It moved the Chiricahuas off their homeland and onto another reservation. The Chiricahuas were miserable. Not only did they have to leave their homes. They also had to live with other Apache groups with whom they were not on good terms.

Once again, the Chiricahuas decided to battle the Americans. They found a new leader—a brilliant warrior named Geronimo. He was such a fierce raider that American newspapers called him "the Apache terror." Geronimo, though, always maintained he

APACHE RESERVATIONS IN 1890

(modern state and international boundaries)

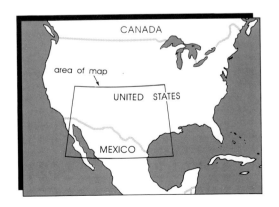

never staged an attack without a good reason. "I never do wrong without a cause," he declared.

Geronimo continued his raids for many years. He was captured by the Americans several times, but always, against great odds, was able to escape. Finally, in 1886, his luck ran out. Feeling his small band could no longer survive against the entire U.S. Army, he surrendered to his enemies. Geronimo's surrender marked the end of an era. The Apaches, once a free and mighty people, had been conquered. ▲

Geronimo and his followers, photographed after their surrender to the U.S. Army.

A group of Apache boys posing with bows and arrows near the Mescalero agency in 1884.

CHAPTER 5

On the Reservation

B<small>Y</small> 1890, the Apache wars were over. Against their will, the Apaches had become reservation Indians. They now lived in five different locations: the Fort Apache and San Carlos reservations in present-day Arizona, the Jicarilla and Mescalero reservations in New Mexico, and the Fort Sill reservation in Oklahoma.

The Apaches' adjustment to reservation life was not easy. They did not like being confined to one area. Longingly, they remembered the days when they traveled whenever and wherever they wished.

Even on their reservations, the Apaches were not free. Government employees called *agents* lived with them. The agents were supposed to make the Apaches give up all their old ways. They also were to encourage the Indians to like whites.

The agents' first step in this mission was to try to make Apache men take up farming, the profession of many white settlers. But the Apaches had little interest in growing crops. To them, the only proper work for men was hunting and fighting.

Eventually, some Apaches did begin to give farming a try. They had little success, though. The soil on most of the reservations was not very good, so it was impossible to produce large harvests.

It soon became clear that the Apaches would not be able to feed themselves. Even so, the government was reluctant to give them food rations. Officials still said the Indians needed to grow their own food and make their own money. But without fertile land or businesses, the Apaches had no way of doing so.

The starving Indians grew sick. Many died. The Apaches at the Jicarilla reservation were particularly hard hit. A large number caught tuberculosis—a deadly infection of the lungs. In 1917, 9 out of every 10 children on the reservation had the disease.

Another goal of the agents was to send Apache youngsters to schools run by whites. At these schools, Indian boys and girls were taught to speak English. They were also instructed in the customs and manners of white people. The teachers tried to make their students abandon all the Indian ways they had been taught by their parents. If they did not, they were often beaten.

This cartoon depicts a starving reservation Indian deprived of his rations by a greedy agent.

In some schools, Indian children were punished by being locked in a room for a long time with only bread and water to eat.

Agents also encouraged the Apaches to become Christians. They were helped by *missionaries*—religious men and women who came to the reservations to teach the Indians about Christianity. Some Apaches accepted the missionaries' message and allowed themselves to be baptized. But most saw no reason to give up their own religion.

In some ways, it was harder to practice the Apache religion on reservations. In the past, great feasts were a part of their ceremonies. But, now, few families could feed themselves, much less a large number of guests. As a result, ceremonies were shorter and held much less often.

But the difficulties of reservation life also gave the Apache shamans more power than ever. Starving and miserable, the Apaches looked to these wise men and women for comfort and guidance. Some, such as Big John and Silas John Edwards at the Fort Apache reservation, had many followers.

Despite the efforts of agents, the Apaches clung to many of their old ways. Still, over time, changes occurred. Unable to survive any other way, many people began to work for wages. At Fort Apache, for instance, men found jobs cutting hay for the U.S. Cavalry's horses and working as cowboys on local ranches.

To find a job, most people moved to the area surrounding the *agency*. A reservation agency was a cluster of buildings where the agent lived and worked. Usually, an agency also included a trading post or stores. As more Indians moved close by, agencies grew up into towns. For the first time, the Apaches became town dwellers.

Wage work also broke up families. In the past, large numbers of relatives lived close to one another. They liked each other's companionship. More important, they all helped each other to survive by sharing work and food. In towns, the Apaches tended to live in smaller households. Just like white families, husbands, wives, and children stayed in the same home, but other relatives—such as aunts, uncles, and grandparents—did not.

Gradually, the Apaches found other ways of making a living. The residents on some reservations found that, even though their land was not suited for farming, it was ideal for raising cattle or sheep. These people became ranchers. In other locations, the Apaches took advantage of woodland

In the late 1800s, Apache school-children were taught to look and act like non-Indians.

areas. They cut down the trees and sold the timber.

These enterprises brought in some money. But still the Apaches remained poor. Their situation was not uncommon, however. Reservation Indians throughout the United States found it almost impossible to make a decent living.

In 1934, the government realized that its efforts to force Indians to live like their white neighbors had failed. Indians on reservations were poor and sick, and something had to be done. The government's solution was the *Indian Reorganization Act* (IRA). This law was meant to help Indians help themselves. It provided funds to allow Indians to start businesses of their choosing. It also permitted Indians to form their own governments. These Indian governments would work with agents to run the reservations.

The IRA helped Indians in many ways. But it did not solve all their problems. After years of struggling to survive, the Apaches would have to work hard to become a healthier, wealthier, and happier people. ▲

Allan Houser, a well-
known Apache artist,
painted this picture
of a buffalo hunt.

CHAPTER 6

The Modern Apaches

The Apaches have had to face many trials in recent years. Each tribe and the residents of each reservation have encountered different problems. But the basic challenge—improving the quality of their lives—has been the same for all.

Poverty has been the greatest obstacle to this goal. Few businesses have opened on their reservations. Therefore, it is hard for the Apaches to find jobs. Without employment, they find it difficult to make ends meet.

After the passage of the IRA, some Apache groups formed their own governments. These governments have worked hard to create new jobs for their people. They have funded many types of businesses. On the Jicarilla reservation, Apaches have found jobs at a government-funded gas station, car repair shop, restaurant, and laundromat. The Mescaleros have invested in a ski run, restaurant, and gift shop. Even more ambitious is their resort hotel—the Inn of the Mountain Gods. Visitors to the inn enjoy a golf course, artificial lake, and a spectacular view of nearby mountains.

The Apaches have also improved their lot by taking legal action against the U.S. government. In the late 1940s, the United States decided it was finally time to settle many of the wrongs it had committed against American Indians in the past. The U.S. government first formed a special group of officials called the Indian Claims Commission (ICC). It then invited Indians across the country to bring their complaints to this body. Several groups of Apaches went before the ICC. They explained that Americans had taken away much of their land without paying for it. The ICC agreed with the Apaches. It awarded them money to compensate them for this loss of land. In one example, the Jicarillas were given almost $10 million in 1970.

The Inn of the Mountain Gods, a resort hotel operated by the Mescaleros, is one of the Apaches' most successful businesses.

Money from the ICC helped Apache governments pay for new business enterprises. In addition, it has allowed them to fund programs to help solve other problems. Improving health care is one of their greatest concerns. Without enough money to buy nutritious foods, many of the Apaches are plagued with health problems. Poor

Apaches also suffer from bad housing. Until recently, many of their houses did not have electricity or running water.

Providing better schools for Apache children is still another concern. Many Apache students have trouble in the class-room. Often, their knowledge of English is not good. Therefore, they do not under-stand their teachers.

On the Jicarilla reservation, the Apaches have fought to change the local public schools. Now the Jicarilla language is taught in their classrooms. The lessons include in-formation about Apache history and culture.

The Jicarillas also can learn about their past from the Jicarilla Museum in Dulce, New Mexico. It displays crafts, such as bas-kets and leather clothing. These are made by the members of the Jicarilla Arts and Crafts Industry. This organization was formed by the Jicarilla government in 1964. Its goal is to preserve knowledge of these ancient crafts for future generations.

Apache governments have also en-couraged their people to practice the Apache religion. Some Apaches are Chris-tians, but most still perform the same cere-monies their ancestors did. (The girls' puberty ceremony is the one performed most often today.) Fewer people now be-

Jicarilla students playing at recess. In school, these boys learn about Apache history and culture.

come shamans. But those who do are well respected by their fellow Apaches.

The world of the Apaches is a combination of the new and the old. They are working to find modern ways of improving their lives—from equipping their homes with electricity to giving their children the best schooling possible. But they also look to the past. From their rich history of struggle and survival, the Apaches continue to draw strength and pride. ▲

CHRONOLOGY

1527	Four Spaniards from Pánfilo de Narváez's expedition arrive in Apache territory
1540s	Spanish explorer Don Francisco Vásquez de Coronado encounters Apaches living at the mouth of the Rio Grande
1848	Mexico loses Mexican War and surrenders to United States a huge tract of land, including Apache country
1851	James S. Calhoun, governor of New Mexico Territory, signs peace treaty with Mescalero and Jicarilla Apaches
1860	The "Cut the Tent Affair" sets off a decade of Chiricahua raids against American settlements
1871	Aravaipa Apaches massacred by U.S. settlers at Camp Grant
1871–72	Apaches granted four reservations
1886	Chiricahua warrior Geronimo surrenders to U.S. Army
1940s	Apache groups seek compensation for their land from the U.S. government
1970	Jicarillas awarded $10 million from Indian Claims Commission

GLOSSARY

agency	a cluster of buildings on a reservation where an agent lived and worked
agent	an employee of the U.S. government responsible for managing a reservation
band	a group of about 200 Apaches who lived and traveled together
breechcloth	a man's garment made of a strip of animal skin tucked between the wearer's legs and held in place at his waist with a belt
Indian Reorganization Act	an act passed by Congress in 1934 that allowed Indian groups to create their own governments and helped fund Indian-run businesses
missionary	a person who sought to teach Indians about the Christian faith
pueblo	a village of clay houses inhabited by the Pueblo Indians
reservation	a tract of land set aside by the U.S. government for use by a specific group of Indians
shaman	a person with the ability to control spiritual power to help cure the sick
tipi	a cone-shaped dwelling made of a wooden frame covered with animal hides
wickiup	a dome-shaped dwelling made of branches and grass

INDEX

INDEX

ABOUT THE AUTHOR

NICOLE CLARO holds a B.A. in literature from Bennington College, where she also studied modern dance. She lives in San Francisco.

PICTURE CREDITS